D1498889

Cellist in Exile

Cellist in Exi[

by Bernard Taper

McGraw-Hill Book Company, Inc.

New York / Toronto / London

a portrait of Pablo Casals

Cellist in Exile

Library of Congress Catalog Card Number 62-18530

62857

PICTURE CREDITS

   Title page, Alan Macmahon; *57*, Library of Congress; *121*, Alan Macmahon

   First gallery: *21*, Puerto Rico News Service; *22, 23, 24, 25*, Dennis Stock, Magnum; *26, 27, 28*, Casals Collection

   Second gallery: *45*, Casals Collection; *46*, Hispanic Society of America; *47*, Radio Times Hulton Picture Library; *50, 52*, Casals Collection

   Third gallery: Solidaridad Democratica Espanola, France, Central Committee; *72*, Casals Collection; *73*, Gjon Mili, Magnum; *74*, Paul Moor, Magnum; *76*, Gjon Mili, Magnum

   Fourth gallery: *93 and 95 bottom*, Puerto Rico News Service; *94 top* and *95 top*, Casals Collection; *94 bottom*, Gjon Mili, Magnum; *96, 97*, Alan Macmahon; *98*, Mark Shaw; *100*, Dennis Stock, Magnum

To Mother

i

EARLY OF A MORNING on a beach near San Juan in Puerto Rico one may sometimes see a rather curious little procession—two dogs, an attractive young brunette, and a small, elderly bald man of stout, invincible build, who carries a black umbrella to shade his eyes from the rays of the tropical sun. They go along the water's edge. The dogs frisk about in the tawny sand. The young woman walks gravely and somewhat solicitously by the side of her companion, who steps along with a quick but rather stiff little stride, and every now and then stops to stretch out his arms and exclaim with delight as he is touched, as if for the first time, by some aspect of nature.

The man is Pablo Casals, taking his ritual morning walk beside the sea he loves, four thousand miles from his native land. In Puerto Rico, at his advanced age, this small powerful figure who is that rarity—an artist with

7

a sense of commitment to humanity—continues, in his own way, to be a source of joy to the world, and a force that sustains and rejuvenates the spirit. At the age of eighty-five he is still playing the cello inimitably. The cello is a hard instrument. Few violinists, even, have been able to go on playing acceptably beyond the age of seventy, and the cello requires not only all the delicacy of control and perfection of ear that a violin does but greater muscular strength. How much longer Casals can continue to play no one dares say at this point. Any performance could well be his last appearance. But on the other hand, Casals being what he is, he might go on to a hundred.

As a widespread musical influence, he is probably at his peak today. The violinist, Isaac Stern, one of the younger generation of performers who have been deeply affected by him, has said, "He has enabled us to realize that a musician can play in a way that is honest, beautiful, masculine, gentle, fierce and tender—all these together, and all with unequivocal respect for the music being played, and faith in it." Though Casals has for more than three score years been esteemed not just as a gifted instrumentalist but as a superior musician, his larger influence dates from 1950, when he emerged from some years of silence and seclusion to take part in the first Casals Festival at Prades, the village in the French Pyrenees where he had settled after the overthrow of the Spanish Republic. On that occasion, and at succeeding festivals a whole younger generation of musicians were exposed to a kind of musicianship very different from the brilliant, electric, antiseptic style which had become established as the predominant contemporary performing style. The pianist Eugene Istomin, who says that everything he now plays shows the effect of Casals' influence on him, has commented, "Casals, by his example and his nature, reminded us of something we had forgotten, or hadn't dared contemplate: the importance in music of color and variety, of feeling, warmth, involvement—in other words, of ultimate human values and meaning."

CASALS has been in self-imposed exile from his native Spain for twenty-three years now, unwilling to accept, even though most of the rest of the world seems to have done so, the Franco dictatorship. Not systematic, perhaps not even always consistent, in the terms in which he has expressed his beliefs, he is nevertheless a man whose moral convictions have shaped his life. His art, Thomas Mann has written, "for all its impetuousness, is allied to a rigid refusal to compromise with wrong, with anything that is morally squalid or offensive to justice— and this in a way which ennobles and broadens our understanding of the artist, placing him out of reach of our irony and setting an example, in our corrupt times, of proud incorruptible integrity."

Casals still considers himself a Spanish citizen. A few years ago, while he was living in France, a French official suggested that he give up his Spanish passport.

Casals replied, "Why should I give it up? Spain is my country. Let Franco give up his passport." Most of Casals' years of exile were passed in Prades, the once obscure village that became world-famous because of his festivals there, but in 1956 he moved to Puerto Rico, where a Casals Festival later sprang up, too. The island was the birthplace of his mother, Pilar Defilló de Casals —a woman of Catalonian ancestry, who left it to go to Spain at eighteen—and also the birthplace and home of Marta Montañez, an intelligent, capable, and personable woman who studied the cello with Casals at Prades and whom he married in 1957, despite a difference in their ages of exactly sixty years. (She is his second wife; his first marriage, which ended in divorce, was to the American singer Susan Metcalfe.)

The sea has always meant much to Casals. He says that his very first memory is of the waves of the Mediterranean, to which he was taken one day as a small child on an outing from his native village of Vendrell, in Catalonia, about forty miles southwest of Barcelona. Some thirty-five years later, when he built himself a house in Catalonia, he chose a site at the edge of the sea at the very place where he first saw it—at San Salvador, just three miles from his birthplace. One of his deprivations during the years at Prades was not living near the water. Now, in Puerto Rico, he has naturally taken a house beside the Atlantic. Situated in Santurce, a section of San Juan, it is a new house of modest size, with white stucco walls and a red tile roof—somewhere be-

tween contemporary and Spanish ranch style in design—
set in a vivid garden of tropical plants and flowering
trees. At high tide, no more than forty feet of strand
separate the house from the water's edge, but Casals says
that if he could he would live even closer to the sea.

Except at the time of the festival, when there are several
weeks of intensified activity, his days follow a fairly
regular pattern during the eight or nine months of the
year he spends in Puerto Rico. (Following the Puerto
Rico festival, he usually travels to Prades for the annual
festival there, and after that he generally goes to Zermatt
and to Siena, where he gives advanced classes in the
cello.) His ways and tastes are, on the whole, rather
simple, though it would be an error to call him a simple
man. Upon returning from his early morning walk, he
invariably plays some Bach to start the day—on the
piano, not the cello, and usually some of the preludes
and fugues. "It is like a benediction on the house," he
says. "I love Mozart, Beethoven, many composers, but
I couldn't possibly begin the day with a Mozart or
Beethoven sonata. It would seem so strange to me." He
breakfasts, and then spends the rest of the morning com-
posing or else practicing on the cello. He still finds new
insights in music he has played countless times, and he
still works out new fingerings for certain passages. "I
have never played a work exactly the same way twice,"
he says, and explains that this is one reason he has
always refused to edit for publication any of the works
he plays, though numerous publishers have sought to

11

persuade him to do so. The story is told of an occasion when Casals, in the course of a lesson, played the opening of the Boccherini concerto to illustrate some point to his pupil. "But Maestro," the pupil said, "that is not how you play it in your recording." To this Casals replied, "No, that may be so, but this time it is the right way to play it." Actually, for Casals, there can be no absolute "right" way to play any work; such an achievement, in his view, would be synonymous with death. Nor does the fact that he discovers new interpretations necessarily mean that he now considers the previous ones "wrong." "When you find a new flower you like," he said once when speaking of this point, "it doesn't mean you have to disapprove of the other flowers you've liked."

In his daily practicing Casals takes care—as he always has—to stop as soon as his muscles begin to grow fatigued, and he advises his pupils to do the same. Moreover, as he plays, he continually and consciously relaxes those muscles that he is not using; he has taught himself to relax finger muscles for the tiny fraction of a second between notes in a rapid sequence. Such habits as these, he thinks, have contributed to his longevity as a performer, though ultimately, of course, the secret of this lies somewhere in his constitution and his will. He doesn't fatigue easily. In terms of physical exertion and dexterity, playing a Bach suite is roughly comparable to chopping down a tree and threading a package of needles at the same time. Casals' wife reports that sometimes of a morning he may sit down with his cello and play a

Bach suite through. "Well, that wasn't so bad," he'll say, and start another. "That wasn't so bad, either," he may remark at the end of the second, and go on to a third. In this way he may play through all six of the suites without intermission, after which he is likely to look over at her, with an expression of mild surprise on his face, and say, "I think I feel a little tired this morning."

Casals' afternoons, after lunch and a siesta, are spent in an attempt to keep up with his correspondence. He tries to answer, by hand, every letter he receives. Casals is honorary co-chairman of the Spanish Refugee Aid Committee, and much of his correspondence concerns the plight of Spanish Civil War refugees, of whom there are still at least a hundred thousand in France alone, many of them living in great poverty and distress. Casals is not a man for abstractions; he commits his emotions directly to whatever engages him. His friends say that more than once, upon stopping in to see him during the afternoon, they have found him weeping at his desk, a letter from one of the Spanish refugees in his hand. His wife has tried to persuade him that not all the letters he receives warrant a personal reply, but she has never succeeded. "Every letter means something human," Casals says. "When a person takes pen and paper and writes to me, he has an idea, a hope connected with me, and at the very least I must respond to this, from common humanity."

In the evenings, Casals may have a few friends in, or he may watch television until he retires, which is usually not much after ten o'clock. On television he likes Westerns best of all. "They are simple and true," he says, "and they repose one." Besides, he may add, they remind him of the America he encountered on his first tour of this country, in 1901. There was still a Wild West then, and Casals saw a good deal of it in a tour which took in all sorts of small towns and way stations. He was part of a trio that included the American singer Emma Nevada and the French pianist Léon Moreau. "Moreau was a high-spirited fellow," Casals recalls. "Together we got into all kinds of adventures and foolishness. For me, that American tour, when I was a young man in my twenties, was a kind of emancipation." In a saloon in Texas he and Moreau became involved in a poker game, in which Casals had the ill fortune to get way ahead, at which point the atmosphere grew decidedly unfriendly. The cardplayers they had taken on, and the bystanders slouching about, were all wearing guns on their belts and looked much like the characters Casals enjoys watching on his screen today. Their dialogue was quite similar, too. When Casals turned down a whiskey offered to him, saying politely that he didn't care to drink while gambling (actually he has never cared much for liquor in his life), one of the others commented in a forceful twang, "Here we play poker *and* drink," whereupon Casals drank. Happily, by drawing on as much skill at poker as he could command, he succeeded eventually in losing his money. All grew friendly once more; they clapped him on the back heartily as he left the saloon and called him a hell of a fellow.

On that same tour, Casals had one adventure that nearly ended his career as a cellist. He was climbing Mount Tamalpais, across the bay from San Francisco, with a party of young people when a boulder came crashing down the mountainside. It narrowly missed his head but hit his left hand—the fingering hand—mangling it severely. At first, the doctors were dubious about his ever regaining full use of it, but after nearly four months of treatment in San Francisco the damage was completely repaired. Casals still recalls with wonder the thought that leaped to his mind the moment after the boulder hit him, as he stared at his bloody hand. "Thank God, I'll never have to play the cello again!" was what he said to himself then—a reaction so complicated that he still does not feel he understands it.

ii

ONE AFTERNOON in the summer of 1961, about a week before the festival was scheduled to begin, I called on Casals in Puerto Rico. I had never met him; the visit had been arranged for me by Alexander Schneider, the second violinist of the Budapest String Quartet, who, among other things, is the assistant musical director, under Casals, of the festival in San Juan. Schneider studied with Casals at Prades, and it was he who conceived the idea of holding a festival there in 1950—the bicentenary of Bach's death—and persuaded Casals to take part in it. A warm relationship exists between the two men; Casals, who has no children of his own, says he thinks of Schneider as a son.

The door of Casals' house was opened to me, after I rang the bell, by Mrs. Casals, who was wearing a flowered dress and earrings of pearl and delicately worked

16

gold wire. She looked very fresh and very poised. When she had greeted me, she said, "Maestro's out on the terrace, working. Would you like to join him there? It's the most agreeable part of the house on a warm day; there's always a breeze." With that, she led me through a large living room to the terrace—a shady, high-ceilinged space, with a wall of red terra-cotta tiles on the garden side and, on the side toward the sea, a wall made of wrought-iron bars, with openings just large enough for the bigger of Casals' two dogs, a boxer, to put his head through to be petted, and for the other one, a small poodle, to wriggle through completely. Casals, wearing a white mesh sports shirt and gray-and-white striped cotton pants, was seated on a small settee, studying a score. He put it aside as we entered and gave me an open and unguarded smile of welcome. Mrs. Casals excused herself, and I started to take a seat across from Casals, but he said, "No, come sit here, why don't you?"—patting a chair beside him. It was the small, spontaneous gesture, I thought, of one who has never been in the habit of keeping life at arm's length. He lit his pipe and drew on it with manifest satisfaction. He is, as is well known, passionately fond of his pipes. Not long ago, when he was asked how much he smokes, he replied, "As much as possible."

We talked for a while about Puerto Rico and the life he leads there. "Is wonderful here," he said. "It contents me. It feels familiar to me. I recognize the countryside, the sea that my mother so often described to me.

She never returned to Puerto Rico once she settled in Vendrell and married my father, but she was often nostalgic for it." His English, though flavored with a moderate accent and an occasional Spanish locution, is fluent, and, like his music, his speech is very expressive. Just the way he utters the word "wonderful" I found to be a lesson in phrasing. The word is sung, with a shape to the dynamics, and there is a slight rubato between the first two syllables. Casals' face, too, is expressive. It is often thoughtful or grave, but even in repose it never seems masklike. When something pleased him during our conversation, his face showed it as frankly as a child's; when he was sad, he did not attempt to conceal it. He has pale-blue eyes and wears rimless glasses. His skin is remarkably smooth, with scarcely a wrinkle discernible. His domed head is bald, with just a fringe of hair—as it has been since he was in his early twenties. His face and body looked somewhat less round and fleshy than I had been led to expect from photographs, and he told me he had lost about fifteen pounds since moving to Puerto Rico. As a result, he now looks younger in some ways than he did in the pictures taken of him during his years in Prades. His gestures as we talked were full of vigor, and I gathered that he had made a full recovery from a heart attack he suffered in 1957, at the first rehearsal for the first Casals Festival in San Juan.

"I used to think that eighty was a very old age, but I don't think so any more," he said to me at one point.

18

"There are times when I feel like a boy. As long as you are able to admire and to love, you are young. And there is so much to admire and to love." He flung his arms up. "Look at the sea, the sky, trees, flowers! A single tree—what a miracle it is! What a fantastic, wonderful creation this world is, with such diversity. That is the law of nature—diversity. That is why I can never play the same work exactly the same way twice, why each note, even, is a different world. My wife says to me, 'You are so excited all the time.' I say, 'I have to be excited. How can I help it?' Teachers should teach this—the richness and diversity and wonder of life. Then there wouldn't be so much *bêtise*—so much stupidity and ugliness—propagated."

I asked him whether he had always viewed the world the way he does now.

"Yes," he said, "I haven't changed much, only developed. I think one becomes formed very early. I was just a boy of thirteen or so when I perceived the awkwardness of the standard cello technique, at least for me, and began developing my own, and it was about the same time that I made the all-important discovery of my life —the Bach suites. Since I was a child, my nature and my outlook have been very much what they are today. As a boy, I was strong and daring but not pugnacious. I didn't much like to fight, but when I finally did, it would be with all my conviction. I never enjoyed having toy soldiers, and when my playmates played at war games I would refuse to join in. Even though I am a Spaniard,

I have never cared for bullfighting—it revolts me. Nor have I ever liked to hunt any living thing. All my life, as far back as I can remember, I have hated lies. When I was seven, I had a bad tooth and had to go to the dentist to have it pulled, and I was afraid to go—fearing not the pain, particularly, but the blood. My father persuaded me—he said it wouldn't make blood. The dentist was a friend of my father's. He, too, assured me it wouldn't bleed. Well, of course it did. I was outraged. 'You didn't keep your word!' I exclaimed. To this day I remember how indignant I was that my father and the dentist had lied to me. Parents shouldn't lie to their children—not even when they think it's for their good. Even a little lie is dangerous; it deteriorates the conscience." Leaning toward me, he put his hand on my arm—a gesture, I came to know, that he makes when he is saying something he cares strongly about—and said, "Conscience—its importance is eternal, like love. Something is happening to the world in this regard. We have consciences still, I think, but we don't heed them as we used to. Personally, perhaps, we still do, but en masse, no. I remember, when I was a young man, the Dreyfus case. The whole world was concerned over the injustice done to one man. Now we are more callous. Millions of people can be killed and we accept it and say it can't be helped."

For a moment, he looked out at the sea with a distant gaze. When he turned back to me, he said, "About myself, you asked—I was lucky. I had, you know, a *won-*

"Zzzau!" he cries as he brings down his baton for a fortissimo entrance.

Reflective appraisal backstage after a rehearsal of the festival orchestra in Puerto Rico—with Alexander Schneider (left), Mrs. Casals, and Rudolf Serkin.

Casals' mother and father,
and the house in Vendrell where he was born.

At the age of five.

derful, extraordinary mother. She was a small, lovely woman—dark-haired, with a fine face. I used to think, when I was a boy, My mother is like an apple! She shaped my moral nature. I don't remember her ever raising her voice, but her way of expression was so imposing that I could not help assenting. She used to say, 'As a principle, I don't respect law.' I and my brother Lluís, when we came of the age at which we were to be taken into the Army, we could pay money to the state and be excused. But that law had been changed when Enric, my youngest brother, came of age—now one could no longer pay to be excused. My mother said to Enric, 'My son, you don't have to kill anyone, and no one has to kill you—go away.' And he went to Argentina." Casals nodded. "That's the way she was—straight." He made a firm line in the air before him with the edge of his palm and repeated, "Straight." He continued, "She was not a demonstrative person. She seldom went to my concerts after I began my cello career. I think she was nervous for me. After the concert, she would say, 'Well, son, were you satisfied?' I would reply, 'Yes, Mother.' And that's all that would be said, even if it was a concert that had been a great success."

December 29, 1876, was Casals' birth date, and it was very nearly his death date as well. He came into the world with the umbilical cord twisted around his neck, blue from strangulation, and it was some time before he drew his first breath. He probably would not have made it at all if he had not been endowed with a rugged constitution. In those days, weak infants didn't survive in Vendrell, where the only obstetrical assistance was provided by the wife of the local coal man. His mother bore nine children in Vendrell, of whom Pablo—or Pau, as he is called in Catalan—was the only one to survive, so that for most of his early years his life was that of an only child. In Barcelona, later on, she was safely delivered of Lluís and Enric. Pau had another close brush with death when, at the age of ten, he was bitten by a mad dog. This happened only a year after Louis Pasteur had administered the first inoculation for rabies, but by good fortune there was some of the anti-rabies serum at a hospital in Barcelona. The boy was rushed there. He was put in a ward with an elderly man who had also been bitten by a mad dog but who had been brought in too late and was dying in agonized delirium. The treatment, which then consisted of sixty-four injections of boiling serum so potent that it frequently caused paralysis, was almost as bad as the disease, but, with the help of a handkerchief he stuffed between his teeth, the boy never once cried out during an injection. "Men don't cry," his father had told him.

Pau's father, Carles Casals, was a short, stocky man of extraordinary physical strength. Of Catalonian peasant ancestry, he was a liberal and anti-monarchist, and he imbued his son with these convictions. The elder Casals played the organ in the village church and added to his meagre income by providing music also for local balls and festivals. It was Carles who gave the boy his first musical training, teaching him the piano, the violin, and the organ. With his own hands, he made Pau his first "cello"—a little, one-stringed curiosity, with a gourd for a sounding board—and he bought Pau a real cello when, at the age of eleven, the boy told him that that was the instrument he most wanted to play. Nevertheless, the father tried his best to discourage Pau from attempting to make a career of music. "Father was a beautiful musician, with a pure, true talent," Casals told me. "He might have been an outstanding composer, if he had had more technical training. But he was a modest man in regard to his talent. He couldn't expect anything big to come from it. He didn't think it was possible for me to make a living from music. He couldn't imagine it, and so he opposed the idea." In fact, Carles Casals arranged to have the village carpenter, who was a close friend of his, take the boy on as an apprentice. Carles himself was skillful with his hands and was of a mechanical turn of mind. He subscribed to scientific magazines, and he and the carpenter used to spend their free time trying to construct various devices he had invented. Though he couldn't imagine his son making a living from music, he could picture himself inventing a flying machine someday. "It was well that I didn't become a carpenter," Casals remarked to me reflectively, as if he were objectively reconsidering the choices that had been offered him. "I am not greatly talented in that direction. It was Mother who insisted that I should follow my bent for music and that I must be given the chance to have expert training. My parents argued bitterly over this. I am afraid I was the cause of much unhappiness between them."

As his mother conceived it, "expert training" meant the Barcelona Municipal School of Music, and when Pau was not quite twelve, she took him to Barcelona, rented a room for them both, and enrolled him in the school. Pau's father reluctantly made the best of the situation; he gave them what money he could spare, but it was not enough to support them. After a few months, Pau got a job playing seven evenings a week in a café trio. The group played the usual café music—waltzes, operatic arias, marches—but Pau persuaded the owner to let him devote one evening a week to a program of classical music. To the owner's surprise, this was a big hit with the café's patrons, and even attracted new ones, including serious musicians—Isaac Albéniz was one of them—who went there specially to hear "El Nen," Catalan for "The Kid," play his cello.

Once a week, Carles visited his wife and son in Barcelona, and often he and Pau would go browsing through music shops. One afternoon, Pau's eyes fell on a volume that bore the title *Six Suites for Violoncello Solo, by Johann Sebastian Bach,* and he says he will never forget the mysterious, premonitory excitement he experienced at that moment, before he had looked at a single one of these works. No one had ever mentioned the suites to him; in fact, neither his father nor his teacher had known they existed. No cellist played a Bach suite in its entirety

32

on a concert program in those days, though occasionally a daring cellist might risk a single movement from one. When Pau got home and sat down to try the suites, he found himself trembling with anticipation. For twelve years, he studied and practiced them nearly every day, discovering in them, as he has since said, "a new world of space and beauty"—and poetry and passion, as well. "The feelings I experienced as I worked on the suites were among the purest and most intense of my artistic life." Only after those twelve years of study of the suites did he finally feel ready to perform any of them in public; and when he did, he revealed them, to the wonder of his early audiences, as a passionate and sublime musical experience, not as the abstract pedagogical exercises they had always been held to be. He is still finding new wonders in them. "For me, Bach is like Shakespeare. He has known all and felt all," Casals said to me. "He is everything. Everything"—he smiled—"except a professor. *Professor* Bach I do not know. When people ask me how I play Bach, I say, 'I play him as the pianist plays Chopin.' There is such fantasy in Bach—but fantasy with order."

At the age of seventeen, having captured first prizes for cello, piano, and composition, Casals graduated from the Municipal School of Music, whereupon his mother decided that it was time to move on from Barcelona. Madrid was next, and there Casals, bearing a letter of introduction from Albéniz, presented himself to Count Guillermo de Morphy, who was adviser and private secretary to the Queen Regent, María Cristina, and was also a patron of music. The Count talked with Casals and heard him play, and was so much taken with him that he arranged for the young man to give a private recital at the royal palace for the Infanta Isabel, the sister of the late King Alfonso XII. Casals' mother was invited to attend, and she brought along Lluís and Enric, not having anyone to leave the children with. In the midst of the recital, Enric got hungry and began to howl. With the Infanta's permission, Señora Casals picked her baby up and nursed him, and in this domestic scene the royal recital proceeded.

Shortly afterward, Casals played for the Queen Regent herself. She, too, was much impressed with him, and granted him a monthly allowance of two hundred and fifty pesetas—about fifty dollars. On this, Casals and his family were able to subsist while he pursued his studies in Madrid—studying chamber music with Jesús de Monasterio and composition with Tomás Bretón. The family lived in a tiny garret, sharing a landing floor with a vivid, noisy collection of poor Madrid folk—some women cigarmakers, a hall porter with a resplendent uniform that was his great pride, a shoemaker with two mentally deficient children. These lodgings were just across the street from the palace, and Casals passed freely from one to the other, neither unduly enraptured by the splendor of the palace nor unduly depressed by the poverty of his own dwelling. During this time the Count de Morphy took his general education in hand. The old Count had

34

been the tutor of King Alfonso XII; the textbooks which young Casals studied from now were the ones that Alfonso had used, with the King's own notes in the margins. The Count had no male children of his own, but he would sometimes say that he had been blessed with two splendid sons—Alfonso XII and Pablo Casals. Every week he required Casals to pay a visit to the Prado and write an essay on some painting that had impressed him, and out of these visits grew a love and appreciation for painting second among the arts only to that which Casals feels for music. For education in affairs of state and also in rhetoric, Casals was expected to attend the sittings of the Cortes and listen to the debates there. His own natural style of speech and thought was much more blunt and direct than the rhetoric favored by the famous speakers at the Cortes, but still he found these sessions absorbing.

On his visits to the palace, Casals sometimes played games with the seven-year-old Alfonso XIII, who was destined to be Spain's last king—a charming, rather wistful child who told Casals on one occasion that he liked music well enough but that what he was really interested in was some cannons for his toy soldiers. Casals gave him some stamps instead. At least once a week Casals performed on the cello for Queen María Cristina; also, since she was an accomplished pianist, they often played duets. More than a patron, she became very fond of him personally. On his visits they would spend many hours talking together. Of the Queen, Casals has said, "This great and gracious lady was a second mother to me." It was an anomalous situation, this warm relationship between a poor Catalonian lad and the Queen of Spain, but the royal favor Casals enjoyed never for a moment made him less a lover of liberty than he had always been or altered his belief in the superiority of republicanism to monarchy. On the other hand, later on, after the Republic was established, he never hesitated to express the gratitude and affection he felt toward the late Queen María Cristina, even though such sentiments had ceased to be in fashion.

When Casals was nineteen, he left Spain for the first time, moving on, with his family, to Brussels and then to Paris, in search of recognition as a musician. Unfortunately, he could not gain access to the people who mattered. In Paris, at a time when he and his family were near starvation, the best he could get was a job as second cellist at the Folies-Marigny, performing can-can music in the pit for four francs a day. After a discouraging winter of that, he went back to Barcelona, became a cello teacher at the Municipal School of Music and principal cellist of the Barcelona opera, and for two years saved up his money until, in 1899, he felt that he was ready to try Paris again. This time, he had a letter of introduction to the noted conductor Charles Lamoureux from Count de Morphy. The story of his meeting with Lamoureux has often been told. When Casals arrived at the conductor's home for an audition, Lamoureux was seated at his desk in his writing room, obviously preoccupied. He muttered his annoyance at being disturbed, and continued writing as Casals prepared to play the Lalo Cello Concerto. As soon as the first notes of the cello sounded, Lamoureux dropped his pen. Owing to a physical disability, he could move his body only with great difficulty. He slowly turned in his chair and laboriously raised himself until he was standing facing Casals—a position he maintained throughout the concerto. When it was over, Lamoureux threw his arms about him. *"Mon enfant,"* he said, "you are one of the elect." He engaged him forthwith to play the Lalo at the Lamoureux Orchestra's first concert of the season, on November 12, 1899.

It was a decisive moment, not only for the performer, but for the instrument as well. Casals was to revolutionize the techniques of bowing and fingering, reveal a range of phrasing, intonation, and expressiveness that had not previously been thought possible, and make the cello an instrument of high purpose. It is strange to recall now that when Casals began his career the cello was not taken very seriously as a concert instrument. "I am not fond of the violoncello: ordinarily I had as soon hear a bee buzzing in a stone jug," wrote Bernard Shaw at about that time, and he went on to deride a repertory that, on the whole, seemed to consist of innumerable repetitions of such things as "Kol Nidre" and Popper's "Papillons." It was Casals who showed the world what the cello could be. "With the advent of Casals a new era may be said to have begun," *Grove's Dictionary of*

Music and Musicians declares in its history of the cello.

On the terrace where we sat talking, the poodle had succeeded, for the fourth or fifth time that afternoon, in wriggling through the bars, and was frisking about us; the boxer put his head in and watched enviously. Casals laughed and patted the boxer's head. I looked at my watch; it was about time to go. "Wait a moment," Casals said to me. "I'd like to show you something." We went into the living room, where he began to rummage in a long low cabinet near the grand piano which took up much of one end of the room. Not finding what he was looking for, he called to his wife, who came into the room and joined him in the search. "Even *you* can't find it," he complained mildly to her, as they looked first on one shelf and then another. "Ah!" he exclaimed triumphantly a moment later, producing a large manila envelope, "here we have it!" As he opened the envelope and took out the contents, he said to me, "These are my treasures." They were letters and original music manu-scripts—and treasures they proved to be. He showed me the manuscript of Brahms' String Quartet in B Flat, Opus 67, and a page on which Mozart had set down the ending of the third act of *The Marriage of Figaro*, then a Mendelssohn letter, written in an elegant hand, and a letter of Beethoven's, with the writing hurled angrily onto the paper. Next, he lingered a moment over a letter of Wagner's. "There's Wagner writing to Auguste Manns —and Manns was the conductor with whom I made my English debut," he said. "I love to think of the continuity of music's history—of musicians passing their heritage on from one generation to the next. I like to think of myself as part of the continuity."

Then Casals took up a single scrap of paper, holding it delicately in both hands. "Here is the one I cherish most," he said. It was a piece of paper from Beethoven's notebook. On it Beethoven had jotted down his first idea for the opening of the Ninth Symphony. It was very close to the idea he finally used, except for one note, which he eliminated. There was also a tympani detail for those bars, which he eliminated, too. Casals stood beside me, studying the scrap of paper. "Think of it!" he said. "Think of what music came out of this!"

iii

I VISITED CASALS several times after that. Generally, I arrived at his house at five and remained for about two hours, and we sat out on the terrace, enjoying the breeze and the vista—the sea and the sky and the flowering trees. Mrs. Casals would stay with us for a few minutes and then excuse herself, rejoining us later on with a tray of refreshments. She is a classic Spanish beauty, with olive complexion, fine regular features and a noble brow. Facially, she bears something of a resemblance to the youthful portrait of Casals' mother, which hangs on the wall of the living room. Indeed, when I first glanced at it, I took it for a portrait of Marta Casals.

She and her husband seemed very warm and affectionate with each other. Sometimes, for some easy and lighthearted give and take, they would slip briefly into

40

Catalan. During her years with Casals, she has picked up this language, and by now, he says, she speaks it very well. As for Casals, though he is fluent in a number of other languages—English, Spanish, French, Italian, German, and Portuguese—it is Catalan in which he expresses himself most completely and naturally. Catalan is for him the language of deepest intimacy. "Why, if I couldn't speak Catalan with my wife, I wouldn't feel I was really married," he once told me.

Catalan, he took pains to stress, is not to be considered a mere dialect of Spanish; it is a true and ancient language in its own right, related to Provençal. "It was the language of troubadours," he said, adding proudly, "and of free spirits." He recited a sentence that the Catalonian people had addressed to their ruler in the Middle Ages and had inscribed in their constitution: "Each of us is equal to you and all of us together are greater than you," and he commented, "That's Catalonia! We were always independent, always free. We were the first people in the world to have a constitutional parliament—even before the British. In the Middle Ages we were a great nation. All the Mediterranean part of Spain, together with southern Italy and Greece—all this was Catalonia in the fourteenth century. But we never had a king then; a count was our ruling figure. That was exalted enough for us; we didn't believe in setting anyone up as a king. We Catalonians have not forgotten we were once a great nation, which is why, though we are willing to be part of Spain, we resent the way we are treated. We are the richest part of Spain. We have always worked hard and produced great riches, yet now if we want to do anything—to put up a little bridge, say, near my village of Vendrell—we have to go to Madrid about it and pay bribes to Madrid officials for permission to build, with our own money, this little bridge. The Catalonians really have a very different personality from other Spaniards. Most like us are the Basques. The Catalonian temperament is very active and hard-working—very honest, imaginative, and idealistic."

He had, it seemed to me, painted a portrait of himself. "And stubborn, too?" I asked.

"Of course," he said. "Very stubborn." He paused, then added, "And musical, especially in singing. In exile, wherever they meet, Catalonians band together, and the first thing they do is start a chorus, an *Orfeó Català*—immediately they sing."

In a radio speech about Casals, the Catalonian composer Roberto Gerhard once said, "There is a Catalan word that, significantly enough, has no equivalent at all in the Castilian [or Spanish] language: the word *'seny.'* It is not exactly 'wisdom,' not 'common sense,' but in its fullest psychological meaning the inclination to take an eminently 'sensible' view of affairs. Casals' art is instinct with that quality; I believe it is the one which has always preserved his art from the dangers of self-willed effects, or from what Paul Valéry has called *'les écarts*

42

personnels.' Indeed when I listen to the calm utterance
of a Catalan peasant or look at his way of tilling the land
with an economy and loving care that reveals an almost
disinterested sense of beauty, or when I behold the fine
architectural simplicity of the most humble dwelling of
the Catalan peasant or fisherman, I feel acutely conscious
of the underlying identity between the human attitude
disclosed in these things and that which one can observe
in Pablo Casals' approach, let us say, to the technique of
his instrument, or to his rendering of one of Bach's unaccompanied suites."

Something of the same sort was said to me on one
occasion by a close friend of Casals' whom I met in San
Juan, a Spanish refugee named Dr. Alfredo Matilla, who
is a historian and a former diplomat, and now teaches
political science at the University of Puerto Rico. "I
think of Casals as the very quintessence of Catalonia,"
he said. "No matter how much fame he has attained, no
matter how many grand personages have made much of
him during his illustrious career, he has remained fun-
damentally a Catalonian peasant. In all countries, I believe, it is the peasants who have been the true carriers
of culture and wisdom. A man can be educated and still
not be cultured or wise. I say this even though I myself
am a city person, and a *Madrileño* at that. The Catalonians all recognize in Casals the essence of the Catalonian
personality. And, of course, in these years of exile he has
been their inspiration. I am sure that if Franco were to

43

fall and Catalonia be granted some form of the autonomy that so many Catalonians strongly desire, they would at once nominate Casals by acclamation to be their President."

In the living room of Casals' house, there is a bust of Casals, and on the wall above it Casals has hung the Catalonian flag, with its four red stripes across a yellow background. (He has hung the flag of Puerto Rico above his mother's portrait, on another wall.) Over the years, I had, of course, heard and read a good deal about Catalonia's importance to Casals, but only in a general way; it was really not until I met and talked with him that I began to comprehend the intensity of his feeling for his native region and realize how deep his homesickness for it must have been during all these years of exile.

His emotional stake in Catalonia is more than simple nostalgia for the scenes of his childhood. During his mature years the region was the focus of much of his efforts and aspirations. For almost two decades before the First World War, he had lived the life of an international concert artist, with Paris as his base. He had attained world-wide recognition as a performer without a peer, who could command the highest fees for his performances, but it did not satisfy him. As he sometimes will say, quoting the Catalonian poet Maragall, "It is on the firm soil of our native land that we must place our feet in order to take flight to Heaven." All those years he had desired to be more closely identified with Cata-

The salon of Casals' villa at San Salvador.

Queen María Cristina, his "second mother."

Paris, 1899—at the time of Casals' debut with the Lamoureux orchestra.

"A legendary trio"—Casals, Thibaud, Cortot—in 1904.

A performance long remembered was the one
Casals, Fritz Kreisler, and Harold Bauer
gave of the Beethoven Triple Concerto in 1917
with the New York Symphony, under Walter
Damrosch. Kreisler is on the left in this photograph, Damrosch seated in the center.

Below, at New York's West Side Tennis Club
during one of his American tours before the
First World War, about 1912. Casals was a
passionate devotee of tennis and took to the
courts every chance he got.

Barcelona, 1927—Casals with the violinist Eugène Ysaye and the Orquestra Pau Casals. This was an historic and moving occasion. Ysaye had been the great virtuoso of the epoch but his powers began to decline while he was only in his fifties. He had not played in public for some time when Casals told him he wished him to come to Barcelona and play the Beethoven Violin Concerto with the Casals

orchestra for the Beethoven centenary celebration. Ysaÿe began practicing scales laboriously like a beginner. His performance contained unforgettable moments. The audience gave him a fervent ovation. Afterward, Ysaÿe fell on his knees before Casals, clasped Casals' hands in gratitude and cried, "Resurrection! Resurrection!"

Some Hausmusik in Vienna in 1933 at the time of the Brahms centenary. The pianist is Ar
Schnabel, the violinist (at right) Bronislaw Huberman, and the violist, Paul Hindemith.

lonia and to be of more use to it, and when the war ended he began spending most of his time there when he was not on tour. (It was then that he settled into his house at San Salvador, a large, classic villa, which was later seized by the Franco régime, but which, after Casals had *in absentia* paid a fine—or "ransom," as he puts it—of a million pesetas, was turned over to his brother Lluís, who now occupies it.)

The most significant fruit of his resolve to devote more of himself to Catalonia was the Orquestra Pau Casals, which he founded in Barcelona in 1920. Barcelona had never had a first-class symphony orchestra; a couple of orchestras were in existence at this time, but they functioned in a desultory and slipshod way—a lamentable state of affairs for a great city, Casals thought. With his own money, he hired eighty-eight local musicians and began rehearsing them, which meant, in effect, retraining them, to overcome the careless habits they had fallen into. "My first preoccupation, knowing the bad habits of orchestral musicians," Casals later recalled, "was to create an atmosphere of artistic endeavor, to awake or reinforce their sense of responsibility and obtain maximum efficiency, so that each player could feel like a soloist." He did not wish to impose his will dictatorially, in the manner of some conductors, but rather to convince his men that what he was asking of them was what the music itself demanded. "I did not mind repeating an explanation as often as necessary,"

53

Casals said. "It seems to me that if the conductor himself is convinced, he ought to find the means of convincing his orchestra."

At first, his rehearsals consisted of hours of a most elementary orchestral exercise, in which the men worked through a single piece of music of the sort they had always glibly tossed off—Wagner's "Ride of the Valkyries." He required them to work through it not merely phrase by phrase but note by note. The results were a revelation to all. In time, the orchestra became an outstanding ensemble and developed into a vital part of Barcelona's cultural life; Casals regularly conducted it in a spring season and a fall season of concerts, and distinguished soloists came from all over the world to perform with it. Eventually the orchestra even managed to become self-supporting, but not before Casals had spent more than three hundred thousand dollars on it. Costly and time-consuming as the orchestra was for Casals, it was also a source of great happiness and pride. During the years when he was concentrating primarily on his cello performances, he once wrote to a friend, "If I have been so happy scratching a violoncello, how shall I feel when I can possess the greatest of all instruments—the orchestra?" He did his first real conducting at the age of sixteen, in Barcelona, when Granados, feeling too nervous to do so himself, asked Casals to conduct the rehearsals of Granados' first opera, *María del Carmen*. In later years he has been guest conductor of some of the greatest orchestras in the world, but that Barcelona orchestra of his—which, of course, has long since been disbanded—will always occupy a special place in his affections.

In Barcelona during the twenties, Casals also helped establish a remarkable institution, the Associació Obrera de Concerts, or Workingmen's Concert Association. Members of this association, upon paying annual dues of only six pesetas (about half a dollar at that time), were entitled to attend six special Sunday-morning concerts of the Orquestra Pau Casals, at which soloists of international repute (including Casals himself) performed. The Sunday-morning programs were not "pops" programs; such condescension would have been offensive both to Casals and to his audience. It still gratifies Casals to recall that the composer most favored by that audience was Bach.

The administration of the association was in the hands of the workingmen, and nobody who earned more than five hundred pesetas a month could belong. Within a few years, its members numbered several thousand and it had established branches throughout Catalonia, many of which—in true Catalonian fashion—promptly formed choral groups. The association had a good music library of its own, and, at Casals' suggestion, it published its own monthly magazine of the arts, with articles contributed by the members. One issue of this workingmen's periodical, which was called *Fruició*, contained pieces entitled "The Relation of Art and Ideas,"

55

"Beethoven and the Late Quartets," "The Intolerance of Art," "Schubert, an Appreciation," and "Stravinsky and Rhythm." Moreover, the association members developed an amateur orchestra of their own. It was homespun but competent. One of its members was a carpenter who had made his own double bass, and who, not having the money for carfare, used to walk from his home to the rehearsal hall—a distance of several miles—with his double bass on his back. To Casals, such a man is an inspiring figure and a true Catalonian. All of these things—the Workingmen's Concert Association, its magazine, and its orchestra—have also vanished.

How the Catalonians felt about Casals in those years can be illustrated by an incident that occurred in Barcelona in 1929, when King Alfonso decided to attend a concert of the Orquestra Pau Casals at which Casals was to be a soloist. Shortly before this, Alfonso had offended Catalonian sensibilities by a speech in which he had identified himself with the eighteenth-century monarch Philip V, who is detested in Catalonia because he deprived the region of its ancient privileges and institutions. When Alfonso entered his box, the audience greeted him icily, but when Casals appeared onstage, the crowd rose and broke into a tumult of cheering. Somebody shouted, "If that one is our king, then Pau is our emperor!" and the cry was taken up all over the hall. It was a scandal, and Alfonso was no doubt affronted. Not many months afterward, however, he made

56

Weihnacht 1913

Pablo Casals

an appeasing gesture toward Catalonia, with Casals once more cast in the role of symbol. The King invited Casals to perform at an official reception at the Palacio de Oriente in Madrid for the King and Queen of Italy, and then, after the performance, while the whole audience of dignitaries, including the Italian royalty, stood and waited, as protocol required, he went up to Casals and chatted with him publicly in the most friendly manner for fully twenty minutes, recalling how they played together in the palace when Alfonso was a boy, and inquiring after his family. The King made only one reference to the Barcelona episode. "Well, Pablo," he said, "I want to tell you how happy I was to see how the Catalonians love you." Both men laughed, in recognition of all that was being left unsaid—these two very different figures whose contrary paths would, within a few years, lead both to exile.

Though Casals has never been a member of any political party, he is republican to his marrow, and the Spanish Republic that came into being in 1931, after Alfonso's abdication, had his strong support, particularly since it restored many of Catalonia's privileges and granted the province considerable autonomy. He saw the Republic as enhancing not merely the freedom and welfare but also the dignity of its citizenry and as bringing long overdue reforms to reduce the disproportionate roles which the Army and the Church had played in the ordinary affairs of the Spanish people. (Though baptized a Catholic at birth, Casals has long since ceased to participate in Catholicism's forms and sacraments. He is, however, a profoundly religious being. "When one looks about at the miraculous diversity of this universe —at the miraculous world that each person, each leaf, is—how can one help but believe in something greater than oneself, that can't be described," he said to me on one occasion. "But,"—with a flash of stubborn pride— "I don't need a church to tell me this. Nor do I believe in confession to a priest. I confess every day—but directly. 'I've been stupid today, oh God,' I say. 'I won't repeat it.' That's how I confess.")

In addition to all else, the Republic was gratifying to Casals in respect to the impetus and encouragement given to popular education and the arts. This happened all over Spain; in Andalusia the poet Federico García Lorca was encouraged by the government to form a traveling theatre and take his poetic dramas from village to village: but in no part of Spain was there a more vital surge of activity in the arts than in Catalonia where, during the preceding régime, the native cultural forms and language had been discouraged. Casals was happy to participate in this and served as the president of the Catalonian government's music council, the Junta de Música, which set out to aid and foster the musical life of the region in a variety of creative ways—establishing musical education in the schools on a far more comprehensive basis than ever before, subsidizing singing

59

societies, providing prizes for Catalonian composers, founding a conservatory.

For its part, the Republic and its citizenry showed Casals much honor and affection during those years. Streets and plazas were named after him. Madrid honored him in a ceremony declaring him *un hijo predilecto,* or favored son, as did many other cities. The most memorable of the civic tributes was undoubtedly that of Barcelona. Over two hundred Catalonian societies and institutions and a large part of the populace participated in an *homenatge a Pau Casals* one evening in 1934, which culminated in a great concert at which Spain's three most distinguished orchestras—the Orquestra Pau Casals, the Symphony Orchestra of Madrid, and the Philharmonic Orchestra of Madrid—all performed. As a mark of the city's esteem, on that occasion a fine, broad thoroughfare in one of the newer sections of Barcelona was renamed the Avinguda Pau Casals.

On the day, in 1931, that the proclamation of the Republic had been celebrated, Casals had conducted his orchestra in a performance of Beethoven's Ninth Symphony before an audience of twenty thousand at the palace of Montjuich, in Barcelona. "The Republic came into being in Catalonia singing Beethoven's hymn to brotherhood and joy." Francesc Macià, Catalonia's first President, once declared. Casals was rehearsing that same symphony one night five years later, for a concert scheduled to take place the next day as part of a "Celebration for the Peace of the World," when a government messenger arrived with word that an insurrection had broken out against the Republic. The musicians had just reached the last movement. Casals told them the news —that an attack on Barcelona was expected at any moment, and that the performance for which they were rehearsing had been canceled. "I do not know when we shall meet again," Casals told them, "so I propose that we finish the symphony now as our farewell to each other." The performance of this movement that ensued remains, for Casals, an unforgettable experience. The symphony is one, in any case, which means a great deal to him. He has said he hopes that when freedom is finally restored to Spain, orchestras throughout the world will mark the event by performing the Beethoven Ninth Symphony.

During the civil war, Casals gave numerous benefit concerts abroad to raise relief funds for the Republic, and he put a large part of his personal savings at the disposal of the government. Though not everything done in the Loyalist name met with his approval—he strongly deplored the bloody violence of the Anarchists and the machinations of the Communists—there was no doubt about his allegiance to the Loyalist cause, and he did not hesitate to proclaim it to Spain and to the world. "How could I, who came from peasant stock, help but be in sympathy with the people, with the Republic? I am an artist but in the practice of my art I am also, after all, a

61

manual worker and have been all my life." As Barcelona continued to hold out, Casals was able to return there from abroad in 1937 and again the following year and give several benefit concerts. One was interrupted, but not terminated, by an aerial bombardment; throughout this violent intermission Casals sat by himself on the stage with his cello, playing a Bach suite. As he talked of the civil war years to me, he broke off with a look of pain on his face so acute that I thought for a moment he was going to weep. "I saw such things there—such things! To this day I can't bear to think of them," he said.

In 1938, in the course of a broadcast of one of his Barcelona concerts, he issued a desperate and prophetic appeal to the democratic nations of the world. First in English, then in French, he said, "Do not commit the crime of letting the Spanish Republic be murdered. If you allow Hitler to win in Spain, you will be the next victims of his madness. The war will spread to all Europe, to the whole world. Come to the aid of our people!" But it was too late—and anyway, the democracies were not listening to such things just then. Barcelona fell on January 26, 1939, and the Spanish Republic came to an end two months later. The day before Franco's troops entered the city, the rector of the University of Barcelona wrote out by hand an honorary degree for Casals; it may well have been his last official act.

Certainly this was to be the last honor Casals would receive from his native land. The new régime erased his name from all the streets and plazas that had borne it, and even took away the plaque that the village of Vendrell had placed on the house where he was born. The broad, handsome boulevard in Barcelona that under the Spanish Republic had been known as the Avinguda Pau Casals was now renamed in honor of one of Franco's generals.

After the fall of the Spanish Republic, Casals sought to take up residence in Paris, but his distress over what had happened to his country and to his hopes for it was too acute to permit him to resume a normal life. "Never was anyone more completely demoralized, both physically and spiritually," recalls the cellist Maurice Eisenberg, at whose home in Paris Casals stayed for a while. "How he grieved for his beloved home, his family, his war-torn country, and the cause for which he had sacrificed so much." In profound despondency Casals lay in his room, with the blinds down, for several weeks, seeing nobody, until at last one of his old friends from Barcelona succeeded in persuading him to rouse himself. "Pau, you must not stay here in Paris like this," he said. "Come back to Catalonia where you can walk in the soft air and hear the sound of Catalan being spoken."

Thus it was that he went to live in Prades, a pretty village at the foot of Mount Canigou which, though it is in France, just across the border from Spain, is part of a thoroughly Catalonian region. There, at first in a room at the town's one hotel, and then later in a tiny house named Villa Collette, he lived through the years of the Second World War. Nearly six hundred thousand Spanish refugees had made their way across the border into Southern France in the last days of the Republic— a terrible odyssey made in the dead of winter. They were interned in ill-equipped camps, where many died. Casals devoted himself to efforts to improve their lot. His hotel room became an unofficial office from which thousands of letters were written, seeking contributions of food and clothing for the refugees. With the truckloads of supplies that had been received in response to these appeals, he would go from camp to camp—Vernet, Septfonds, Rivesalte, Argeles, and others—doing what he could to sustain his compatriots, in body and spirit. The plight of those among the surviving refugees who have never been able to find adequate employment or who have been ravaged by illness still preoccupies him. "I have them always in my heart," he says. "They have shown such dignity, such nobility, despite all that has happened to them."

With how much hope Casals greeted the end of the Second World War! The world seemed full of promise and, though nearly seventy, he was eager to get back to his music and to performing in public once again. "Now that the Germans have gone," he wrote to a friend at that time, "I have resumed my practicing and you will be pleased to know that I am making daily progress."

Along with many other people, Casals had assumed that victory for the Allies would automatically mean the end not only of Hitler and Mussolini but of their supporter Franco. As the months went by, however, it became painfully apparent to Casals that the democracies had made a decision, for reasons of diplomatic expediency, not to press for the restoration of free government in Spain. In the autumn of 1945, to protest this policy of the democracies toward Spain, Casals broke off a concert tour he was making in England. From his personal standpoint, as a cellist, it had been as triumphant a tour as he had ever made. The ovation with which he had been greeted at his first appearance in the Albert Hall had been more tumultuous than any that could be recalled. The critics could not find superlatives enough to describe his playing. Honors and acclaim were being showered upon him. But his misgivings over what he felt to be the moral betrayal of the Spanish people's hopes for liberty were growing all the while. Profoundly disillusioned, he announced that he could not in all conscience go on concertizing as if nothing were amiss. He had stopped playing in Germany from the time Hitler began persecuting the Jews, and he had given up playing in Italy not long afterward. In those instances, he had felt that he could not separate his behavior as an artist from his beliefs and ideals as a human being. The same thing, he felt, was the case now. Retiring to Prades, he

65

vowed that he would not play again in public until Spain was liberated.

Casals is neither a systematic philosopher nor a politician. Certainly, he hoped his action of protest would have some effect on the world, but he was not, by this means, attempting to lead any political movement or even to establish a standard of behavior that others would be expected to follow. He has never felt he had the right to prescribe how other artists should comport themselves. When the conductor Wilhelm Fuertwaengler came to Casals after the war, bearing letters from Jews he had helped, and sought to justify himself to Casals for having continued to conduct in Berlin throughout the Nazi régime, Casals told him, "It is quite unnecessary for you to give me an explanation, as I cannot interfere with anything one way or another."

Casals believes that each person must act according to the dictates of his principles. Of such actions as his protests against dictatorship and his decision to give up playing in countries which recognized Franco, Casals has said that his main motive has been to enable himself to live at peace with his own conscience. "One's actions are a part of one's existence," he once said. "One feels it a duty to act, and whatever comes one does it—that's all—a very simple thing. I feel that the capacity to *care* is the thing which gives life its deepest significance and meaning."

Over the years since 1945 he has modified the letter of

the vow he made then, but essentially in a way that furthers its central purpose and reinforces his moral position. Consistently he resisted all efforts of impresarios to entice him back to the performing circuit. (One American concert agency sent him a signed blank check and authorized him to fill it out for whatever fee he might care to name.) When, in 1950, he finally did emerge from retirement for the Prades Festival, on the occasion of Bach's bicentenary, it was not to fulfill a commercial engagement. Nor, as a cellist, has he fulfilled such an engagement to this day. Many of his admirers and friends, though honoring his moral stand, have felt he took too extreme a position in renouncing his art for so many years. During a meeting with him in 1951, Albert Schweitzer observed, "It is better to create than to protest." To this, Casals replied, "Why not do both—why not create and protest, both?" This is perhaps the position he has achieved. Every time he now plays, at one of his festivals or on some other extraordinary occasion —at the United Nations in 1958 or at the White House in the fall of 1961, for example—the world is reminded of the situation he continues to protest.

Beyond that, his activities in recent years have been motivated by the urgent compulsion to draw the world's attention to the menace posed by the nuclear arms race, the problem which increasingly preoccupies him and disquiets his soul. He expressed this in the words he addressed to the United Nations, when he performed before that forum: "If at my age I have come here for this day, it is not because anything has changed in my moral attitude or in the restrictions that I have imposed upon myself and my career as an artist for all these years, but because today all else becomes secondary in comparison to the great and perhaps mortal danger threatening all humanity." He wished, he went on to say, that there could be a tremendous movement of protest in all countries which would impress those who have the power to prevent the catastrophe that looms over mankind. This is the cause in which he now seeks, by such means he has at his disposal—his music, his words, his prestige— to be of some service to mankind during the years that remain to him.

Conscience—its importance is eternal . . ."

In a terrible odyssey in the dead of winter some six hundred thousand refugees fled into France across the Pyrenees when the Spanish Republic fell. "I have them always in my heart," Casals says. In his room at Prades he spent hours every day, writing letters all over the world beseeching aid for his unfortunate compatriots.

In the church at the first Prades festival—Casals conducting a performance of the Bach A Minor Violin Concerto, with Isaac Stern as soloist.

"It is better to create than to protest," said Albert Schweitzer. Replied Casals, "Why not do both—why not create and protest, both?" This photograph, taken in Zurich in 1951, caught the two men at the moment of this exchange.

A rehearsal at Prades,
at the abbey of
St. Michel de Cuxa.

A Prades concert, with Serkin at the piano.

iv

INJUSTICE, CATALONIA, LIBERTY, PEACE—these were the
recurrent themes of my conversations with Casals. And
music, of course, and people he had known through a
long life span, and nature, and the celebration of life.
His powers of memory continually amazed me. Once I
showed him a fifty-year-old snapshot of him on a tennis
court, which I had found. He supplied me at once with
details of date and place. I asked if he recalled with
whom he had been playing. "The violinist Dethier," he
promptly replied. "Did you win?" I asked. Casals
laughed and said, "Yes." He was easy to be with. He
not only talked well but, as I found whenever I had ob-
servation or anecdote of my own to offer, he also listened
well—a much rarer trait in a famous old man. The cello,
too, loomed large in our conversations, though it did not
dominate them. At one point, in response to a question

77

of mine, he expatiated on what had been the most important of his revolutionary innovations in cello technique. "Mainly, I simplified cello technique, made it more natural," he said. "I freed the arms. Formerly cellists played in a very artificial posture, all cramped up. They used to keep their elbows close to their sides. Teachers made their students hold a book under the bowing arm while practicing, to develop this habit. The violinists used to do the same. Look here, I'll show you." We happened to be in the living room at the time—Casals, his wife, and I—and he rose from his chair and led me over to a corner of the room where a small colored drawing hung on the wall. It showed the nineteenth-century virtuoso Joachim playing the violin, accompanied at the piano by Clara Schumann. Joachim was dressed in black, with a flowing cravat. His hair was long and in tempestuous disarray. His head was flung back in ecstasy, his eyes half closed. He was romanticism personified. But for all that, now that Casals had drawn my attention to it, I could see that he looked piteously constrained, with his arms pinned to his sides, as if he were held in a straitjacket, and with only his wrists and fingers free to move. "You see how they played," Casals remarked. "I couldn't play like that. It never made sense to me. So I developed a free, natural use of the arms. Like this." He made soft, wafting movements with both arms, a gesture that suggested to me not so much a cellist playing his instrument as a bird soaring gently in a tranquil sky. "See?" he said happily, as he wafted. "Free—natural."

This change, Casals said as he resumed his seat, was not only a technical improvement, in that it was less tiring than the old way and enabled the performer to play with more strength, control, and variety of effect, but also a spiritual improvement, because it liberated the performer's musical personality. "And then the hand," he continued. "In fingering, cellists used to move constantly the hand. They would hold the hand like this" —he illustrated in the air with a cramped claw of a hand—"and keep sliding it up and down. I opened the hand, enlarged and extended the reach—like this." His right forearm became a cello's neck, on which the left hand took up its fingering position. With the hand itself stationary, his fingers reached out here and there on the imaginary strings. "I could play now four notes without having to move the hand, whereas before they had been able to play only three. Everything is easier, and phrases can be much better sustained. It's really a very simple thing, what I did with the hand, but nobody had ever thought of it before. My teacher was, of course, scandalized when he saw me playing this way—for, as you know, I was only thirteen when I began developing my own technique of playing—but he came to accept it when he saw the results I got. He was, by the way, a very fine teacher, and a wonderful person."

"Occasionally, Maestro still gets a pupil who has

79

learned the other way of playing," Mrs. Casals said. "All cramped up, and sliding his hand up and down the cello's neck. And then Maestro will say to him, to this pupil who may be sixty or more years younger than he is, 'Ah, I see you belong to the old-fashioned school.'"

Book-length treatises of a technical nature have been written by musical pedagogues to present and explain, for the benefit of other cellists, the detailed implications of Casals' system of cello playing. In these works one finds Casals credited with numerous other discoveries of a radical nature, in addition to those he had mentioned to me. One such is a carefully worked-out system of fingering, based on the principle of the extended reach, which for the first time made it possible for a cellist to play with a fleetness and facility approaching that of a violinist. Another is a percussive manner of striking the strings in fingering, with the fingers curved and raised high and thrown like hammers at the strings—a technique rather similar to that used by Spanish guitarists. Casals' method creates, as one authority has written, "an extraordinary sense of vitality and precision." Still another discovery, of central importance to the quality of Casals' playing, is "expressive intonation." Depending on the melodic and harmonic context, some notes will be slightly sharped, others slightly flatted. Hungarian gypsy violinists have long done this instinctively, but Casals was the first to systematize the practice.

These technical improvements were developed by Casals with "irrefragable logic" in response to the basic

80

question he always asks when confronted by a musical problem: "What is the most natural way of doing this?" As Juliette Alvin wrote in the *Musical Times* some years ago, "The whole of Casals' technique is based on music. Its scientific beauty arises from the fact that he has discovered the exact meeting point of the musical needs of the artist, the physical possibilities of the hand, and the inherent nature of the instrument. . . . This perfect relation between the body and the cello explains why Casals' playing never seems to be a work of physical toil, even when his muscles are working to their utmost."

For all his spontaneity as a performer, Casals has, all his life, consciously explored every aspect of his craft. "Many of Casals' disciples mistake him when they take his emphasis on feeling, intuition, and freedom to mean a lack of discipline," Isaac Stern has said. "There's no such self-indulgence in his approach to music. 'Honesty to the limit' has been his lifelong motto, both as man and as musician. He himself is stubbornly disciplined. He has worked painstakingly through the most minute details of technique and conception, and it is because he has done so that in the end the details become less important than the grand design. His is a discipline in the service of a liberation—that's the crucial thing." It is because he has always known exactly what he was doing to achieve any given effect that he has been able to pass on his discoveries to others. Very few great performers have possessed this talent. Maurice Eisenberg has written a revealing account of Casals as a teacher in the music

81

publication *Violins and Violinists:* "How well do I recall my first lesson with him," he writes. "I had played the concerto of Schumann with the Pau Casals orchestra in Barcelona under his direction, and I was looking forward to playing it again at my lesson to get his detailed criticism. Before I had a chance to begin, he asked me to sing the first note, a sustained E. I did this. 'Good,' said he. He then requested me to conduct the note as though holding a baton. He asked me if there were fluctuations or curves in the line of the note when I sang or conducted it. I of course answered in the negative. 'Then why did you use curves in your wrist and bow action when playing it on the cello?' he inquired. These few words—which Eisenberg cites as an example of Casals' "simple, profound logic"—came as a revelation. Eisenberg says he pondered them for several days, and by the next lesson found that he had managed to get rid of all superfluous movement and that his technique had undergone a complete change.

My own best insight into Casals' cello techniques and his way of communicating them as a teacher derives, not from the books I have read or even from my conversations with Casals, but from a series of films I have seen, showing Casals teaching a master class of advanced cello students at the University of California in 1960. A series of twenty-five films produced by Nathan Kroll for the National Educational Television and Radio Center, this documentary, which has justly won international awards, permits a layman such as I to share, in an intimate and spontaneous way, the experience of being a student under Casals—gleaning from the master a wide range of musical pedagogy, from such revelations as the architectural shaping of a Beethoven sonata to practical hints as to how to make as much noise as possible in a certain passage of the Dvořák concerto, where the orchestra is playing fortissimo and will drown out all but the most vociferous of cellos.

I mentioned having seen this film to Casals and he looked pleased. "Ah, then you've seen the way I teach. The aim is to follow the musical truth. I sit facing the pupil with my cello and I play as much as I talk, or more —giving the example together with the general. I like very much to teach, for I have always learned much myself while doing so. I would like to continue to pass on my ideas about music to young people as long as I am able."

After a little more talk about cellists and cellos, I asked Casals about the special characteristics of his own instrument. "I'll go and fetch it if you'd like to see it," Mrs. Casals said. "When Maestro's not using it, it's kept in the only air-conditioned room in the house."

"For myself, I do not care for air-conditioning," Casals said. "But for the instrument it is necessary, because the atmosphere is so damp here in Puerto Rico. Even so, the sound is affected. It does not sound so pure here as it does in Europe. Violins are affected here, too, but not so much, because they are smaller."

After a moment, Mrs. Casals returned to the room with

83

the cello, which was draped in a fawn-colored cloth. "Thank you, *maca*," Casals said, using a Catalan term of endearment, as she removed the cloth and gave him the instrument. He sat holding it between his knees, in the familiar playing position. "My cello is a Goffriller, made at Bergonzi's house," he said. "It was made in 1733, I think. It has not a big sound—not as big as the sound of Stradivarius cellos, some of which have a personality that I find too strong, too dominating for my taste, even though very beautiful—but though not big, the sound that this one makes is very equal, and as an instrument it is very convenient for me, because it is not too large. It's a bit smaller than the average cello." He glanced down at his cello, whose neck reposed in his left hand. Plucking a string lightly, he added, "It's a lovely instrument, this one, with its own personality. I have played on it for over fifty years, and I wouldn't change. It is my old friend, my lifelong musical companion. I would recognize its voice in the dark anywhere, just as one would recognize the voice of a dear old friend."

With that, he held his cello out for me to look at. He held it horizontally, with both hands under it. Its lines seemed to me graceful but not delicately so; it had a sturdy, workmanlike air, for all its grace. On its dark-reddish-brown surface, which glowed with a soft sheen, I could see small scars and worn places here and there. I felt very conscious of the years it had lived. After a moment, I glanced over at Casals, who had also been

84

contemplating his cello, a little introspective smile on his lips. He caught my eye and his smile broadened. He nodded vigorously, as if to sum up whatever he had been thinking, and then he handed the cello over to his wife, who draped it in its cloth and carried it from the room.

Casals took up his pipe, filled it, and lit it. As he leaned back in his chair, smoking contentedly, I remarked that the strings of his cello seemed quite worn.

"Ah, yes," he replied. "The more worn a string, the better it sounds. And do you know when it sounds best of all? Just before it's about to break. *Le chant du cygne.*"

I asked if that didn't present a hazard in concerts.

"Very much so!" he affirmed cheerfully. "But that's just one of the risks you have to take. I remember a recital once in Geneva. I was playing the Sixth Bach Suite. Everything went well—the prelude, the allemande, the courante—until I came to the sarabande. It's a very difficult movement, with double stops, and just after I started it, the A string broke. I retired and changed the string, while the audience waited. Returning to the stage I began the suite over again from the beginning. It's very hard to play with a new string, but again things went quite well until I reached the sarabande. There, at the very same place, the new A string broke."

"How strange!" I said. "What did you do then?"

"Well, I retired, again put on a new string, came back onstage and started a different suite. I understood by then that the Sixth Suite wasn't for me that day."

v

As a composer, Casals is less well known and less fervently acclaimed than he is as a performer, but he has written music nearly all his life. When he was seven, his father undertook to provide the music for a Christmas pageant—"Els Pastorets," or "The Adoration of the Shepherds"—that was to be presented in their village, and, finding himself with several sections of the pageant unfinished as Christmas drew near, he called on young Pau to help compose what remained to be done. Pau, who had sung in tune before he could talk, had already proved himself competent at harmony and complicated transpositions, and in his family it was taken for granted that the son of the house could lend a hand in writing music, just as in the carpenter's household across the lane a child of that age might have been put

86

to work helping his father build a kitchen cabinet. Since that first effort, Casals has composed in many forms. He has written symphonies, oratorios, quartets, sonatas, and songs, but not much of his work has been performed or published. He says he has not wished to force his compositions on the world on the strength of his reputation as a performer. "If, after I die, the world should discover that it likes what I have written, well and good," he said to me. "I compose because I like to compose." A few of his works have been published by the Benedictine monastery of Montserrat, however, and in 1960 a chorus of Catalonian exiles gave a performance in Acapulco of an oratorio of his called "El Pessebre," or "The Crèche" (a subject that would seem to have brought him around full circle to the "Els Pastorets" of his childhood). Casals composed this in Prades in 1943 and 1944 to a poem by Joan Alavedra, a Catalonian poet. At the time he composed it, he had intended that it should receive its first performance in Barcelona after the fall of Franco, but years have passed and he is no longer as confident as he once was that he will outlive his country's dictator or that he will ever again see a free Spain. The work has subsequently been performed in San Francisco and New York, with Casals conducting, and other performances are to take place later on in Europe. Casals says he would like it to be sung throughout the world—including Russia. He says he thinks of the work as "a message of peace" and that proceeds from performances of it are to be used to promote the cause of world peace. The name "Pau," incidentally, means "peace" in Catalan.

During one of my visits, Casals offered to play a tape recording of the Acapulco performance of his oratorio for me. We took chairs into the foyer, where the phonograph is, and sat down to hear the tape. Eyes closed and pipe in mouth, Casals listened intently to his music. Before long, he was conducting the performance, with a burnt match as his baton. Sometimes he stamped his foot to bring on the crescendos; sometimes he sang through his pipe. The tape was an amateur transcription—blurred, scratchy, and uneven. Outside, a violent thunderstorm broke. The rain drummed on the roof and the trees could be heard being lashed by the wind. What with the storm, the bad tape, and Casals' stamping and singing, I doubt if I was able to give the oratorio a discriminating hearing—though the total impression, as can be imagined, was most vivid. The music, or what I was able to hear of it, had something of an old-fashioned quality, with harmonies that satisfied the expectations they aroused, and with unmistakably resolved cadences. Instead of cleverness, that characteristic virtue (and vice) of contemporary works of art, it unapologetically offered sentiment.

At the end of the recording, Casals looked over at me and commented, with great satisfaction, "Back to music, eh? Back to music!"—meaning that he felt he had returned to the true musical language. I was, of course, aware of his aversion to contemporary music; it has been frequently expressed. He feels that the patterns of sound created by modern composers, while often curious and ingenious, have no relation to the great tradition of music and do not touch the emotions of the listener in the way that music always has. It happens that this point of view is not shared by many of the soloists and orchestra members who perform with Casals at the festivals. Most of these musicians are young, vigorous, and sensitive, and though these are qualities that Casals cherishes in them, the same qualities dispose them to be keenly receptive to musical experimentation. But they are grateful to Casals for all that he has to offer them in the rich realm that is music to him, and feel no need to quarrel with him over this other territory. "It's not really so surprising that Casals doesn't like modern music," a member of the festival orchestra remarked to me later. "Modern music is apt to be intellectual and non-melodic. For Casals, melody is life itself, as you can tell by his playing and by what he is always trying to bring out when he conducts. As a person, he is so vibrantly alive and so responsive to everything about him that one might think he would also keep up with modern music, the way Stravinsky has, but he's a very different kind of being from Stravinsky. In a way, despite his life and vitality, Casals remains a nineteenth-century figure—one of the last of the nineteenth-century giants. Even his

89

political liberalism and morality are those of a bygone epoch, which is perhaps why they speak to us with such poignancy."

Apropos of all this, the musician went on to tell me of an episode that had occurred a couple of years ago. "Occasionally, during these festivals, Casals has had a bunch of us over to his house for an evening," he said. "We sit around and ask him questions and listen to him talk and reminisce. My God, what wonderful evenings those are! Well, one evening, one of the fellows in the orchestra began trying to persuade Casals that he ought to like modern music. He kept on pressing Casals, rather—asking him, 'How about the Bartók quartets,' and how about this piece and that one? The rest of us got quite annoyed with him. It seemed so pointless. After all, we were lucky enough to be with a man who had so much to give us in regard to music—a man who could tell us how Joachim played, who had known friends of Brahms, who had talked with Dvořák and Rimski-Korsakov and Debussy about their own works—so why waste time on one of the few areas where Casals could not contribute? Finally, Casals ended the discussion by saying, 'Sasha Schneider hears these modern pieces as beautiful. You hear them as beautiful. You are fine musicians, and if you hear it, there must be something there. All I can say is that I don't hear it. I don't hear any music there.'"

vi

THE FESTIVAL that year was the fifth since Casals' arrival in Puerto Rico. Whatever the island's charms, it possessed no tradition of classical music before Casals moved there, but in these recent years a musical life of considerable importance has sprung up. In 1958, acting on Casals' recommendation, the government established a conservatory of music. Casals, who is the president of the institution, took an active part in formulating its basic plans, and his wife teaches cello on the faculty. It is housed in a new building in San Juan and has attracted a student body of almost two hundred. In addition, a Puerto Rico symphony orchestra has been formed. It is small, but a few of its players are of high enough calibre to be included in the superb festival orchestra that assembles in San Juan in the summer. The Puerto Rico symphony has taken to touring the island, playing the classics of symphonic literature in the open squares of little towns, where a live symphonic work had never before been heard. For all of this, Luis Muñoz-Marín, the Governor of Puerto Rico, is deeply grateful to Casals. Shortly before Casals arrived, Muñoz had launched what he called Operation Serenity, to counteract the baleful effects on the island's cultural life of Operation Bootstrap—the economic program that has fostered hundreds of new industries in Puerto Rico, and at the same time has threatened to spread a gaudy, jukebox culture over the island. Muñoz hadn't dared hope for assistance from a figure of Casals' stature, and he has accepted it as a godsend; anything that Casals suggests the island may need in the way of musical training or activities the government eagerly supports. Even before any of this had occurred, Muñoz-Marín, as a man of culture (he is himself a poet) and a libertarian, had been inclined to regard Casals with some awe. On Casals' eightieth birthday, Muñoz-Marín thought it would be fitting to have his name spelled out in lights on a great electric display, the *Fuentes Fluviales,* that the Puerto Rico Water Resources Authority maintains on the Condado Lagoon in San Juan. The director of the authority said, "But Don Pablo is still alive," and reminded the Governor that such displays were only put on in honor of some historic personage. To this, Muñoz-Marín replied, "Don't you know the difference between someone simply alive and an immortal?"

As the opening date for the festival drew closer, I

In 1956, shortly after his arrival in Puerto Rico. His living room walls are hung with souvenirs and mementos. "I like to have my things out where I can see them," he says.

Two pictures that Casals treasures. Above, a photograph autographed by the Casals Festival orchestra in 1957—the year he suffered his heart attack—when the orchestra, out of tribute to him, went on to present a remarkable series of concerts without a conductor on the podium. Below, a last visit with his old friend, Fritz Kreisler, in 1958.

Above left—making a fine point to the pianist Eugene Istomin after a concert. Right, with Dag Hammerskold on the occasion of Casals' eventful concert at the United Nations in 1958. (Below), with Governor Luis Muñoz-Marín.

*Casals as teacher—three candid photographs
taken during a master class he gave
at the University of California in 1960.*

Mark Shaw;

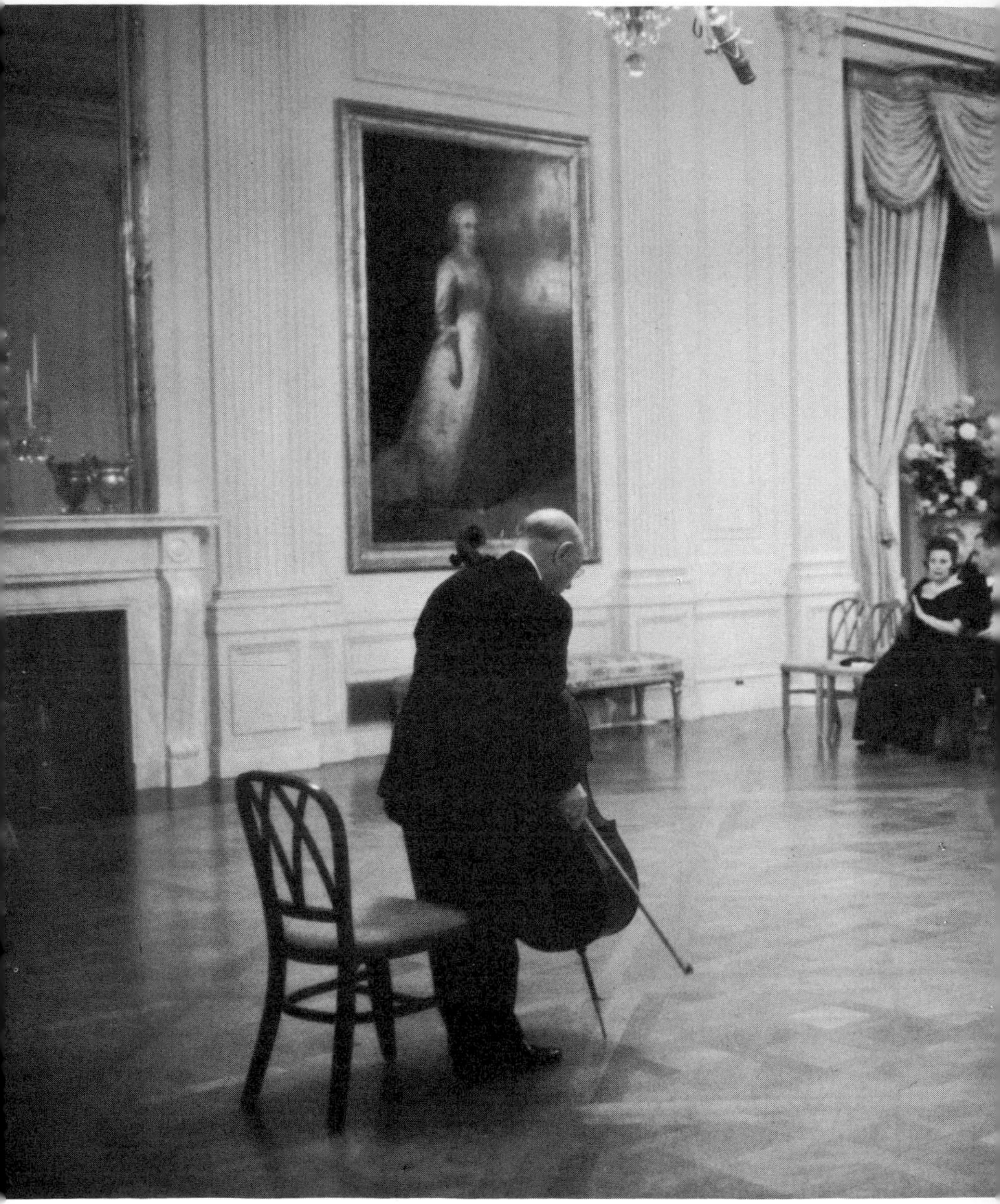

At the White House,
November 13, 1961.

became aware that preparations for it were beginning to take an increasing amount of Casals' attention. One afternoon when I called at his house, I found him and Alexander Schneider, who is a vigorous-looking man with a leonine head and a shaggy mop of grizzled hair, seated side by side at one end of the living room, scrutinizing a sheaf of papers and discussing, in French, various decisions that had to be made. Casals' cello, draped in its cloth cover, reclined at an angle nearby, its neck resting on a chair in front of the piano. After we had exchanged greetings, I left them to continue their discussion and joined Mrs. Casals, who was seated a few feet away. She was conversing with a tall, fragile, rather elegant white-haired lady, who, I learned, had just arrived in Puerto Rico for the festival. Her name was Mrs. Thérèse Jelenko. She was from San Francisco, and I was interested to learn that she had first met Casals back in 1901, when he made his first tour of the United States, and that, indeed, she and some young companions had been with him on the memorable outing to Mount Tamalpais that nearly put an end to his career. "I was walking just in front of Pablo," she recalled. "The rock went right past my head. I didn't have time to shout before it hit him." During the ensuing months in San Francisco, where he stayed at the home of Gertrude Stein's parents (at a time when Miss Stein was still unknown) while his hand healed, Mrs. Jelenko saw him often, she said. "We had a lot of fun. I was just seventeen years old then, and Pablo was twenty-four. I must

101

frankly confess that I became his shadow. He was a very romantic figure." At this rather winsome confession on the part of her elderly guest, the young Mrs. Casals responded with an understanding smile.

A few moments after this, our conversation was interrupted by a burst of laughter from Schneider, one of his characteristically robust laughs, with head flung back, his hair flying. He turned to us and said, "He's been practicing the Schubert B-Flat Trio already—this far ahead of the concert! He says he's nervous about a passage in it."

"Oh, yes," said Casals seriously. "Very nervous. Is very difficult." He walked over to his cello, removed the cover, and sat down in the chair, with the instrument between his knees. Bow in hand, he sang the concluding notes of the part taken by the violin just before the cello makes its entrance in one section, and then he began to play the cello part. His hands trembled, his eyes looked frightened, his body was tense. From his cello came a line of ragged, wavering, uncertain Schubert.

Schneider roared with laughter at this parody of anxiety. "You know," he said, "if I were mad at you, I could do like this—" He sang the same violin part in an abrupt and perfunctory manner. "No preparation, see!" he said, cocking his head at Casals. "But I'm not mad at you, *cher maître,* so I'll give you the preparation, don't worry." He thereupon sang the violin's phrases once more, this time with a humorously exaggerated retard as an obvious cue for the entrance of the cello.

Casals nodded, acknowledging the musical joke but looking very wistful. "You can give all the preparation you want," he said, in a sad voice, "but I still have to play the passage." He lifted his bow, and, his face now thoughtful—or, rather, wearing that expression of serene concentration one often sees in photographs taken of him while he is performing—he addressed himself to his instrument. The Schubert passage now emerged with immense beauty. Phrase upon phrase, the melodic line unfolded like a flower coming into bloom before one's eyes. There seemed not the slightest shadow of anything problematical or troublesome about the passage. At the end of it, Casals paused, his bow hovering above the strings. Then he played it through again, with the same beauty. He sighed as he concluded, letting his bow arm fall to his side. "Is very difficult," he said gloomily, and then stood up and draped the cover over his cello.

The episode set them to talking about the nervous anxiety that nearly all performers, however experienced or famous they may be, undergo when they play in public. Schneider said that one of the few he knew who were not affected in this way was the pianist Mieceslaw Horzowski. "When he has a concert coming up, he just takes it in stride," Schneider said. "It amazes me how he can be so calm. I remember one day, though, when he confessed that he hadn't been able to eat all day, worrying about the performance ahead of him. Rudolf

Serkin was there when he said it, and he was delighted to hear it. 'Good!' Rudy said. 'Now you know how the rest of us feel all the time.' "

Casals laughed, as we all did. Then he said soberly, "Is no joke, that anxiety. Is a terrible thing. I have always, when I go out on the stage to play, a pain here." He put his hand over his chest. "I always say to myself, 'Why should it be so?' But it is so. All my life it's been like that. I remember that even as a little child, when I had to play my violin studies for my teacher, I would get that terrible anxiety. I think it's unusual for so young a child to get anxious over playing, don't you?"

Both Schneider and Mrs. Casals disagreed with this. They said that, to judge by their own memories and what other performers had told them, the painful uneasiness over performing was a trait that showed up very early in those who later proved talented. It seemed as if it were almost a necessary aspect of precocity, like absolute pitch. The child who didn't suffer in this way, they felt, was very lucky, yet probably didn't have the temperament to become a great performer.

"It's strange that one never gets over this condition, not even when one gets to be as old as I am," Casals said. "It's worst of all when I am playing solo. When I play a duet with a pianist, there's less pain, and still less when I play with a chamber group. I can share the responsibility with the others then. Best of all, for me, is when I don't play at all but conduct."

As I listened, I found myself contrasting these un-

104

happy revelations of a lifetime of distress in the service of music with something that Casals had said to me just the day before. "I thank God to have been a musician!" he had exclaimed. "It has been a great privilege, a great joy." The painful emotions connected with public performance—an anxiety deriving, apparently, from an acute sense of responsibility to a standard or conception of performance far beyond what was necessary to win the applause of the public and the critics—do not cancel the joy a performer such as Casals finds in making music. But for Casals, as for many other performing artists, it has always been a relief and a release to be able to experience the joy of informal, spontaneous sessions. I recalled a vignette I had once read in the memoirs of the English music patron Edward Speyer, at whose country home Casals had been a frequent weekend guest during the first decade of the century. "I remember," Speyer wrote, "his arriving one lovely summer morning in a white flannel suit with a tennis racquet under his arm and announcing, 'Now six sets of tennis first, then the two Brahms sextets.'" I thought also of those remarkable musical sessions, described in a biography of the late Fritz Kreisler, in which Casals took part during the summers just before the First World War. In addition to Casals and Kreisler, they included Georges Enesco, Jacques Thibaud, Ferruccio Busoni, and Eugène Ysaye—a whole galaxy of stars of the epoch. At the end of the spring concert season, they would hurry from wherever they had been performing—from

America and all over Europe—and would gather at Thibaud's house, in Paris, and for hour after hour, liberated from all the pressures, limitations, and distortions of a concert performance, they would give themselves up to playing chamber music for the sheer joy of it.

Schneider and Casals had gone on to talk about the petty things that can plague and distract an artist during a performance. Schneider recalled an occasion in Baltimore when he had been scheduled to play a program of unaccompanied Bach suites—the most demanding program in a violinst's repertory. He had been so nervous before the concert, he told us, that he could eat nothing all day but tea and toast. And then, when it came time to dress, he found that he had neglected to bring along the studs—"buttons," he called them—for his dress shirt. He dashed out of the hotel to buy some, but he couldn't find a store open anywhere in town. Finally, he borrowed a set of studs from the hotel waiter, though they were not quite the size and shape he was accustomed to wearing. "Do you know," Schneider related, looking at us unhappily, "the whole concert those buttons were on my mind. Here I am, playing this sublime, this tremendous music of Bach, and all I can think about is buttons."

There was laughter at this. Casals asked, "You couldn't play *without* buttons?" and then was reminded of something that had happened during his 1901 tour of the United States. One afternoon, he and the pianist Léon Moreau had decided to go and see what a coal mine was like. "It was most fascinating down there in the mine," Casals related. "We got so engrossed we completely forgot we had a concert to play that night. When we finally remembered, we just had time to rush to the concert hall from the coal mine, without even being able to stop and change our clothes or even to wash our faces. You can imagine how we looked." He smiled at the memory. "Pennsylvania was where that was," he added, after a moment. "In—" He considered for a few seconds, eyes closed. "In Weelkspar, I think." Turning to me, he asked, "Is there such a town as Weelkspar?"

Yes, I replied, with admiration for a memory that could dive down sixty years into so rich a past and find the exact little pebble of fact it sought, there is indeed a Wilkes-Barre.

vii

THE NEXT DAY—a Sunday—the sixty-two members of
the orchestra, which had assembled in New York, flew
into San Juan, and the morning after that came the first
rehearsal. Like the concerts themselves, the rehearsals
are held in an auditorium on the campus of the University of Puerto Rico, in San Juan. The auditorium is
Spanish Renaissance in style, with dramatic color con-
trasts and draperies on the walls and convoluted columns
that remind one of masterpieces of the candlemaker's
art, and it holds about two thousand people. Its acous-
tics are quite good, except for a few dead spots down-
stairs; the *cognoscenti* usually sit in the balcony.

At that first morning's rehearsal, the orchestra members had already spent an hour working, under Schneider's direction, on the Haydn Symphony No. 97 when
Casals arrived. They rose to their feet as he walked

108

onstage, and he motioned to them to resume their seats. Since he had greeted them individually the day before at the airport, he simply said, "Is wonderful you are here —and I am glad I am here, too. Now let us play the Schumann." With that, he raised his baton and brought it down vigorously, and the orchestra launched into Schumann's Fourth Symphony. Before the musicians had got beyond the opening note, which is a sustained chord, Casals interrupted them, rapping with his baton and calling out, "Very well! Very well!"—a locution that, as I came to recognize, meant that things were not very well. He wanted the dynamics of the chord shaded differently—with a more rapid diminuendo from fortissimo to pianissimo—so as to give the chord a more mysterious portent, and also to enable the pianissimo theme played by the second violins to be heard more clearly. I saw Schneider, who was now in the concertmaster's seat, exchange glances with the first violist, and from their expressions I guessed that the import of their silent message was something like "Oh, oh! Here we go for an entire rehearsal on the opening chord!" As a conductor, Casals has the reputation for being willing to work with patient firmness at a detail until it satisfies his conception, regardless of the time it may require.

As it happened, it took the musicians only a couple of tries to achieve the effect Casals was seeking. "Good!" he exclaimed, beaming, and on they went into the Schumann, with Casals asking for this or that interpretation as they progressed. He continually rejected mechanically perfect readings, reminding the musicians that every phrase, every note, should have a natural color and expressiveness. "In every note is heart," he said at one point. "Yes, in every note is heart." A sophisticate would never be caught saying a thing like this, but Casals even put his hand to his own heart as he said it. More than once, he urged the musicians not to confuse literalness with fidelity. "Although it is written as you have played it, it does not sound well," he told them at one point in the third movement. "We must do a little something more. Don't be faithful to the notes, be faithful always to the *music*—be faithful to Schumann. Don't be afraid to feel! Trust your feelings!"

His communication with the orchestra was achieved in a variety of ways, none of which appeared studied and some of which even looked awkward in their artlessness. The gestures of his arms and hands were not, in themselves, a study in poetic grace, as they are with some conductors; nor did he seem interested, as some do, in giving a choreographic interpretation of the music there on the podium. Often he would let the orchestra know the quality he sought in a passage by singing it in a hoarse, passionate voice. Sometimes he tried to convey it by means of speech. Words being what they are, what he communicated that way was often only a hint or approximation of the thing he was after, but there were occasions when the words he found were unmistakably evocative. At the start of the second movement, for instance, Casals stopped the orchestra and said, "Now

at this part I must hear the second violins' rhythm"—
he indicated it with his arms—"which gives the—the
anguish." The next time they played the passage, there
it really was—the anguish.

To indicate legato effects, he would often sweep an
imaginary bow back and forth across his forearm. For
fortissimo entrances, he would wind up and cry "Zzzau!"
as he brought his baton down, looking like Zeus hurling
a thunderbolt. He was supposed to sit, while conducting, on a typist's chair that had been placed on the
podium, but he was off it more than on. He appeared
to me to be using the springy seat of the chair the way
a canny fighter uses the ropes—to bounce off when he
needed momentum. (Later on, at one of the festival concerts—one in which Casals conducted this Schumann
symphony—I happened to sit just a few seats away from
one of the heart specialists who had treated Casals when
he suffered his attack. The doctor's face, as he watched
his elderly patient, reflected a mixture of admiration,
apprehension, and awe.) At the end of the rehearsal,
when Casals put down his baton, the musicians broke
into applause; it was applause that, I thought, expressed
their own pleasure in what they had done as musicians
that morning as well as their appreciation of Casals. As
the orchestra members filed out of the auditorium to a
row of buses waiting in a side alley to take them back
to their hotels, they were animatedly discussing the interpretation of the Schumann that Casals had just extracted
from them. The symphony is part of the standard reper-

111

tory, but some were saying that, as often as they had played it, there had been things brought out that morning that they had never heard in the work before. They seemed exhilarated, like skiers coming off the slopes after their first run of the season. "*This* is the way to make music, isn't it!" one of the oboists said.

Enthusiasm is not characteristic of orchestra musicians. They often tend to be, at best, matter-of-fact about their work and, at worst, blasé, jaded, or cynical. For various reasons, many develop a kind of protective shell behind which they can remain spiritually aloof while their fingers and lips execute the required tasks with the highest degree of skill. One of the instrumentalists—a first-desk man in a great American orchestra—commented to me after a concert, "When I arrived here, I was at the point where I was actually hating music. But after just one rehearsal with the Old Man I found I could hardly wait to go off and get at my practicing again."

I came to know a number of the musicians quite well in the course of the festival. They often talked with me about what it was that affected them so deeply in San Juan: Casals' personality, of course, and his superb musicianship; the high standards they were expected to measure up to, standards of expressiveness as well as skill; and, in general, the ambience of dedication, of utter immersion in making music as beautifully as possible, simply for the satisfaction of doing so. A rehearsal under Casals they found to be a memorable experience in itself, not merely a preparation for a public display.

I got the impression that Casals and all the rest of them would have rehearsed with the same devout and joyous concentration even if no public concerts were to follow. I remarked on this once to the pianist Rudolf Serkin, who was a soloist at the festival, as he had regularly been in years past. Serkin said, "That was exactly the situation last summer when Casals spent several weeks in Marlboro, Vermont, at the music school I have there. There were no public performances to speak of, but Casals rehearsed the small student orchestra in various works with the very same love and care."

If anything, the enthusiasm of the orchestra members grew, rather than diminished, as the festival went on. When I would ride in the bus back to their hotels with them after a rehearsal or concert, I would hear them talking eagerly away about the music they were playing and Casals' illumination of it and how marvelous the orchestra was sounding and how, perhaps, this year it was the best it had ever been. They would go on in this vein while having a drink in the bar, or while sunning themselves on the beach during the afternoons off. Once, even, on looking into the gambling casino of the Caribe Hilton, I found several of them standing with their backs to the gaming tables, still animatedly talking music.

To a number of the musicians it comes as a revelation of some intensity to discover, under Casals' influence, how much they still really care about music. More than that, some say that Casals' example, both as a musician and as a human being—his "willingness to love

113

and be loved," as Isaac Stern puts it—affects them beyond their playing. They find themselves making larger gestures, and in general being more open and expressive, more ardent, more receptive. Liberation of the emotions has its dangers, of course—especially to those who have spent a lifetime cultivating indifference. I was told about one blasé violist who came to Puerto Rico to play in the orchestra one summer and then declared that he would never come again and put himself in such mortal danger of being "contaminated" by enthusiasm.

Some of the musicians have been playing under Casals every summer since the first Prades Festival was held. Among them are many exceptionally fine performers. The orchestra, which is assembled annually by Schneider, after consultation with Casals, is, in fact, an ensemble of virtuosi. "It is the cream of the cream," Casals boasted to me. "The least member of the second-violin section could solo in the Brahms Violin Concerto." Quite a few of them are soloists in their own right, or members of well-known chamber groups. Several are first-desk men from such eminent institutions as the New York, Philadelphia, Cleveland, and Pittsburgh orchestras, and some of these—such as Abraham Skernick, the first violist of the Cleveland Orchestra, and Bernard Z. Goldberg, the first flutist of the Pittsburgh Symphony—willingly take second-desk positions in the Casals Festival orchestra. Casals speaks of the orchestra, and of the soloists who come together for the festivals, as "the family"—a confraternity of kindred souls. When he greeted the orchestra at the airport, he could be heard saying warmly to one man, "Now the family is together again." In this particular family, all the members are well aware that he is patriarch. It is not a democracy, but neither is it a tyranny. Casals' authority is rarely questioned, but it is exercised in an atmosphere of mutual respect and understanding. An incident that occurred during a rehearsal of the Beethoven Triple Concerto particularly impressed this on me. For the cello, incidentally, this is one of the most taxing and ungrateful works in the symphonic repertory, the cello's part being pitched almost entirely in the extreme upper register of the instrument; that a man of Casals' age could carry it off as he did, is little short of miraculous. Quite possibly this was the last performance of that work that he will ever give. At the rehearsal I spoke of, there was a pause after the first run-through, with the soloists and the orchestra remaining in place on the stage. Casals bent over his instrument and thoughtfully went over the introductory section to the largo movement, where the cello has the leading voice. He played this through several times, trying to satisfy himself in some regard. Somehow, the last time, the orchestra sensed that he had now worked things out to his satisfaction and would go on. Spontaneously, without any signal that I could discern, the orchestra picked up its part—a pianissimo accompanying theme—and came in behind the cello. The movement swept on, carrying everybody along, as if on a flood tide of music.

Strong as the rapport is between Casals and the orchestra, an even more powerful bond unites him with the great performers who join him in playing chamber music. I was privileged to witness this during a trio rehearsal in which Casals, Schneider, and Serkin took part; I happened to be in the wings just as they were about to go onstage, and, at Serkin's request, went along and turned pages for him. They played through a Haydn trio, then the Schubert B-Flat Trio, and the Beethoven "Archduke." In the wings, they had been chatting and joking, but once they settled down to the music, hardly a word was spoken. It was as if they had gone beyond language. They didn't stop to work on technical matters, but a couple of times they went back and repeated a whole movement. Between works, Casals would sit in contemplation for a few moments, as if basking in the music just played. "Lovely, lovely," he murmured after the Schubert. After the "Archduke," he said, spreading out his arms, "How big! My God, what music! Is incredible!" He turned to Serkin and Schneider, and the three looked at one another with appreciation and gratitude and great affection. Casals embraced Schneider and then Serkin. Then, taking up his cello, he walked, with his short, stiff stride, into the wings.

viii

I WAS NOT able to remain in Puerto Rico till the very end
of the festival that summer, but before I left Casals invited me out to his house for one last visit with him. It
was a Sunday, and there was no concert or rehearsal that
evening; the invitation was for the usual time of five
o'clock. Usually when I saw him, Casals looked vigorous
and hearty, but on this occasion I found him looking a
little worn and rueful. He was soaking his right thumb
in a basin, for an infection had developed in it over-
night, as a consequence of a fingernail's pressing into
the flesh while he gripped the bow—a rather common
misfortune, he said, and added that the cello was an instrument that was not kind to the flesh. There have been
some occasions, he recalled, when by the end of a concert the whole fingerboard was bloody.

That somehow led him, for the first time in our

acquaintance, into talking about the heart attack he had suffered in 1957—the pain, the terrible nausea, and the acute fear. It had come just as he was starting to conduct a rehearsal of the Schubert "Unfinished" Symphony. "You know," he said, "to this day I am scared to conduct the 'Unfinished' again." After ten days, the doctors pronounced him out of danger. A month later, he was allowed to hold the cello but not bow it. Five days after that, though, without any doctor's say-so, he picked up both cello and bow and began to play. "And here I am, playing still," he said.

He was reminded then, by a shift of association, of a fine old pianist he had known. He spoke of him nostalgically. "His name was Planté, and I played together with him in Lyons once. He was around ninety years old then, and still played amazingly well. Of course, the piano is not nearly so hard as the cello or any of the other stringed instruments, but still he was a wonder. He said to me, 'I invite you to play with me at the concert I will give on my centenary.' But, alas, that never took place, for he died at ninety-five."

Casals' reminiscent mood did not last the whole of that day's visit. It gave way shortly to another mood, one in which he was thinking of all the things he still had to do in the world. He mentioned that he had been corresponding with President Kennedy, and he showed me his letters and the President's. They were in a manila folder, which Casals had labeled, in pencil, "Kennedy." Casals had tried to persuade the President to condition future aid to Spain on "an agreement for the re-establishment of freedom and human dignity" in that country. The President, in his reply, paid a respectful and friendly tribute to Casals as a person but did not deal specifically with Casals' proposal, asserting instead a general statement about free government as a basic element of America's credo. Casals professed to find some encouragement in Kennedy's words, however, and spoke warmly of the President as a human being and a statesman.

Casals spoke also to me at that time of his then forthcoming concert at the White House—that celebrated event which, when it took place on November 13, 1961, before an invited audience consisting of composers and other musicians, proved a triumphant and moving experience. More than a mere concert, it was a historic occasion, revealing the esteem in which artists would be held by the Kennedy administration. It was no accident that the first such event to be held at the White House in many years should have Pablo Casals as its principal figure. As President Kennedy said that evening, "The work of all artists—musicians, painters, designers, and architects —stands as a symbol of human freedom, and no one has enriched that freedom more signally than Pablo Casals." As for Casals' performance that night, Paul Henry Lang of the New York *Herald Tribune* was to write, "It is difficult to describe this venerable artist's music-making —to judge with detachment the generous, persuasive and unintentionally dominating nature, and the exuberant

119

though disciplined mind of this octogenarian. His delivery is simple, direct and economical; the bow never quivers, the wondrous sound never falters—we are given the immediate movement of the mind. The music pours forth from his magnificent instrument with a depth of strength that gives a strangely still and tranquil beauty to its agitated emotions. . . . Whether legato or staccato, the tone was luminous and magnificently on pitch. This great artist is one of those musicians that are found once in a century."

Meanwhile in Puerto Rico, more immediate concerts pressed on him that summer—the concerts at the festival —and, in spite of his infected thumb, he was preparing to resume practicing when I left that evening at the end of my last visit with him. His wife urged him not to. "I must," he said. "You have to do your best. If you're going to perform, you have to practice."

They saw me to the door. I shook hands with Mrs. Casals. Casals bade me goodbye warmly, with an *abrazzo* —the customary Latin embrace of salutation and farewell. His cheek, resting momentarily against mine as I bent over him, seemed as delicate as a child's; but his broad back felt as solid and enduring as a great rock.